E-COMMERCE ANALYTICS UNLOCKED

Harnessing Data to Understand Customer Behavior & Increase Sales

Danielle Mead

CONTENTS

INTRODUCTION

Before I founded Duck Soup E-Commerce, I worked for several e-commerce startups. In all of those roles, I was responsible for analytics. This was before Google Analytics, back when I had to run manual sales and traffic reports and combine them into a large spreadsheet that I would distribute to the higher-ups in the company. I loved looking at all the numbers, especially because e-commerce is one of the few industries where you can make a change in your strategy today and then be able to see whether it worked tomorrow.

Running those reports instilled in me the importance of analytics when it comes to e-commerce success. What I learned was that it wasn't enough to just look at the numbers. You needed to pick one or two metrics and focus everything you do on improving them – every day. Even incremental increases in a conversion rate or average order size can mean significant improvements in your company's revenue or profit.

I also learned that you really can't rely on intuition or gut feelings when making decisions about marketing, inventory, pricing, or customer experience. The most successful e-commerce brands leverage data to optimize every aspect of their business – from understanding customer behavior to predicting future trends and fine-tuning their marketing efforts.

Ultimately, the biggest difference between struggling and thriving online stores is their approach to data. Those who track and analyze key metrics consistently make smarter, more informed decisions that drive revenue growth. Unfortunately, many store owners either ignore their data altogether or don't know how to interpret it effectively.

In this book, we'll look at how to collect actionable data for your e-commerce store, and how to leverage it to improve your business.

Common Mistakes Store Owners Make with Data

One of the most common mistakes I see is focusing on vanity metrics – numbers that look impressive but don't directly contribute to business success. Metrics like total website traffic or social media likes may seem encouraging, but they don't always translate into sales. Instead, track actionable insights, such as conversion rates, customer lifetime value, and average order value.

Another common issue is failing to set up proper tracking and analytics from the start. Without accurate data collection, e-commerce businesses are essentially operating blind. If you're starting a new business, set up analytics before you launch. Waiting until you decide to "look at the numbers" means you won't have any data to review – analytics programs will only track your data moving forward.

In addition, I've worked with many clients who didn't realize that their Google Analytics setup was incorrect, leading to months (or even years) of incomplete reports. Traffic data is almost meaningless if you can't see associated conversion and revenue metrics for those referral sources. That's why I always review a client's analytics tools to make sure they are correctly configured when auditing an online store's performance.

Key Analytics Tools for E-Commerce

There are many analytics tools available, each offering unique insights to help store owners make data-driven decisions. Here are a few of the ones most commonly used by the e-commerce clients I work with:

Google Analytics: A must-have for tracking website traffic, user behavior, and conversion rates. It provides deep insights into how customers find and interact with your site.

Shopify Analytics: Built into Shopify, this tool gives store owners essential reports on sales, customer data, and product performance.

BigCommerce Analytics: Similar to Shopify Analytics, but tailored to BigCommerce stores, offering insights into customer behavior, product sales, and revenue trends.

Glew: A more advanced analytics platform that integrates with multiple data sources, providing detailed insights on customer segmentation, inventory trends, and profitability.

I always recommend that businesses choose tools that align with their specific needs and technical expertise. The key is not just having access to data but knowing how to interpret it and use it to drive strategic decisions. In the next section, we'll dive deeper into the types of data e-commerce businesses should focus on to maximize their success.

SETTING UP ANALYTICS FOR YOUR ONLINE STORE

Setting up analytics properly is one of the most important steps for any online store. Without the right tracking systems in place, you really don't know what's happening in your store. You're unable to measure the impact of your marketing efforts, understand customer behavior, or identify areas for improvement. I've seen many e-commerce businesses struggle simply because they didn't take the time to set up proper tracking from the start. In this section, I'll walk you through the basic steps of establishing a solid analytics foundation for your store.

Google Analytics Setup for E-Commerce

Google Analytics is one of the most powerful and widely used tools for tracking website performance. Setting it up correctly for e-commerce is essential to gaining deep insights into customer behavior and conversions.

Step 1: Create and Configure a Google Analytics Account

Go to Google Analytics and sign in with a Google account. Click on Admin and select Create Account to set up a new property for your online store. Choose Web as your data stream and enter your website details. Select Enhanced E-commerce in settings to enable deeper e-commerce tracking. Copy the Google Analytics tracking code and add it to your website's header.

Step 2: Enable E-Commerce Tracking

Google Analytics provides two levels of e-commerce tracking: Basic e-commerce tracking, which records transactions and revenue, and enhanced e-commerce tracking, which provides detailed reports on shopping behavior, product performance, checkout activity, and more.

To enable these features, navigate to Admin > E-commerce Settings in Google Analytics. Toggle on Enable E-commerce and Enable Enhanced E-commerce Reporting.

If you're using a platform like Shopify or BigCommerce, integrate Google Analytics directly within their analytics settings.

One thing I've found useful is setting up custom goals and funnels to track key actions, such as when users add items to their cart, reach checkout, or abandon a purchase. This data can help you pinpoint where customers drop off and optimize your store's user experience.

Setting Up Tracking Pixels (Facebook, Google Ads, etc.)

Tracking pixels are small snippets of code added to your website to track user interactions. They are necessary for marketing campaigns and understanding how effective your paid ads are.

Facebook Pixel

The Facebook Pixel helps track conversions from Facebook and Instagram ads, retarget visitors, and optimize ad performance.

Go to the Meta Business Suite and select Events Manager. Click Connect Data Sources and choose Web. Select Facebook Pixel and follow the instructions to install it manually or via a partner integration (Shopify, BigCommerce, WooCommerce, etc.). Use Pixel Helper (a Chrome extension) to verify if your pixel is working correctly.

Google Ads Conversion Tracking

To track conversions from Google Ads, in Google Ads, go to Tools & Settings > Conversions. Click New Conversion Action and choose Website. Set up conversion categories such as purchases, sign-ups, or add-to-cart actions. Copy the provided conversion tag and add it to your website's thank-you page or use Google Tag Manager for easy integration.

Make sure to test these pixels using their respective diagnostic tools. Over the years, I've seen many businesses lose thousands of dollars in ad spend due to improperly installed tracking pixels.

Understanding UTM Parameters for Tracking Marketing Efforts

UTM parameters are small pieces of code added to URLs to track traffic sources, making it easier to see which marketing efforts are driving results.

How UTM Parameters Work

A standard UTM-tagged URL looks like this:

https://www.yourstore.com/product?utm_source=facebook&utm_medium=cpc&utm_campaign=spring_sale

This tells Google Analytics:

utm_source = Facebook (where the traffic comes from)

utm_medium = CPC (cost per click, meaning a paid ad)

utm_campaign = Spring Sale (the specific promotion running)

You can manually create UTM links using Google's Campaign URL Builder, or just add the necessary code to your URLs using the format shown above. You can also use tools like UTM.io to keep track of your links efficiently.

Best Practices for UTM Tagging

Be consistent: Establish a naming convention to avoid data inconsistencies.

Use UTM tags for all paid campaigns: Whether it's Facebook Ads, Google Ads, or influencer marketing, tracking every source helps measure ROI accurately.

Monitor in Google Analytics: Navigate to Acquisition > Campaigns to analyze how each marketing source performs.

One mistake I see often is store owners not using UTM parameters for their email marketing campaigns. Without UTM tags, all traffic from emails might appear as "Direct Traffic" in Google Analytics, making it impossible to measure email performance.

***

Setting up analytics and tracking correctly is not just a one-time task; it requires ongoing monitoring and optimization. I always recommend checking your data weekly to ensure everything is recording properly. If something seems off – like a sudden drop in reported conversions – it's worth investigating your tracking setup immediately.

By properly configuring Google Analytics, setting up tracking pixels, and utilizing UTM parameters, you'll gain a comprehensive view of your e-commerce store's performance. This will empower you to make data-driven decisions that boost conversions and optimize your marketing efforts. In the next section, we'll explore the different types of key metrics you should be tracking to measure success effectively.

KEY E-COMMERCE METRICS EVERY STORE OWNER SHOULD TRACK

Tracking the right e-commerce metrics is crucial for the long-term success of an online store. I've worked with countless e-commerce businesses, and the most common mistake I see is store owners getting overwhelmed with too many metrics, so they end up tracking nothing. The key is to select a few metrics that directly impact revenue and profitability. In this section, we'll cover the essential e-commerce metrics every store owner should track (and some optional ones), and how to use them to make smarter business decisions.

Website Traffic Sources and Trends

Understanding where your website traffic comes from is fundamental to optimizing your marketing efforts. Not all traffic is created equal. Organic search traffic, which comes from search engines like Google, is often the most valuable because it's free. Paid traffic, from platforms like Google Ads and Facebook Ads, can be a major revenue driver but must be closely monitored to ensure a strong return on investment. Social media traffic can vary depending on the platform and your audience, with some businesses finding great success on Instagram or TikTok while others perform better on Facebook or Pinterest. Direct traffic, which occurs when users type your website URL directly into their browser, is often a sign of strong brand awareness. Referral traffic comes from other websites or influencers who mention your brand, and it can be an excellent source of new customers. And don't forget email marketing, including any automations or flows you've set up.

To get the most out of your traffic data, I always recommend setting up Google Analytics UTM tracking. This allows you to see exactly which campaigns and platforms are driving the most valuable visitors. Having this level of insight helps you allocate marketing resources more effectively.

Conversion Rates: How to Measure and Improve Them

Conversion rate is one of the most important e-commerce metrics because it directly affects your bottom line. A small increase in conversion rate can lead to significant revenue growth without increasing traffic. To calculate conversion rate, divide the total number of orders by the total number of visitors and multiply by 100. For example, if your store gets 10,000 visitors per month and 300 of them make a purchase, your conversion rate is 3%.

Improving conversion rates requires a multi-faceted approach. Optimizing product pages with clear descriptions, high-quality images, and customer reviews can make a significant difference. A streamlined checkout process, where unnecessary steps are removed and multiple payment options are offered, also plays a key role in boosting conversions. Additionally, abandoned cart recovery emails can help bring back shoppers who left items in their carts without completing their purchase. Finally, experimenting with different pricing strategies and promotional offers can provide insights into what resonates most with your audience and encourages them to complete their purchases.

If you're looking to improve your conversion rate, it's also worth comparing your shipping and return policies against your competitors every so often. Shoppers hate paying for shipping, so if your shipping rates are higher than other websites, or your competitors have free shipping and you don't, shoppers might be deciding to abandon their orders. Strict return policies, such as only offering store credit instead of a refund, can also deter shoppers from buying from you.

Average Order Value (AOV) and How to Increase It

Average order value (AOV) measures how much

customers spend per transaction. It is calculated by dividing total revenue by the number of orders. For instance, if your store generates $50,000 from 1,000 orders, your AOV is $50.

There are several strategies to increase AOV. Upselling and cross-selling are two effective techniques, where customers are encouraged to purchase a premium version of a product or add complementary items to their cart. Bundling products together at a slight discount can also entice customers to spend more. Another effective strategy is setting a free shipping threshold, where customers are incentivized to increase their order size to qualify for free shipping. Loyalty programs can also drive higher AOV by rewarding customers who spend more with exclusive perks or discounts.

Additional Metrics to Monitor

Beyond traffic sources, conversion rates, and AOV, there are a few additional metrics that I like to track. Revenue Per Visit shows how much revenue each visitor generates, and reflects both your conversion rate and your average order size in one single number. This metric helps assess whether you are attracting the right audience and if your website experience is effectively converting visitors into paying customers.

Lifetime Customer Value (LTV) is another helpful metric that predicts how much revenue a customer will generate over their entire relationship with your business. To calculate LTV, multiply the average order value by the purchase frequency and customer lifespan. By increasing customer retention through email marketing, subscription models, and loyalty rewards, you can significantly improve LTV and long-term profitability. After all, retaining existing customers is always less expensive than acquiring new customers.

Finally, Average Items Per Order is a useful indicator of whether customers are purchasing multiple products in a single transaction. To encourage higher numbers, store owners can implement bundling strategies, volume discounts, or suggest related products during checkout. When customers purchase more per order, overall profitability improves without needing to acquire new traffic.

***

Tracking these key metrics will help you make data-driven decisions that improve profitability. Rather than getting lost in a sea of numbers, focusing on the right insights will provide a clear picture of what's working and what needs improvement. I recommend picking one or two metrics to optimize against – making sure that all of your design and marketing efforts are intended to improve them over time.

UNDERSTANDING CUSTOMER BEHAVIOR THROUGH DATA

One of the most valuable aspects of e-commerce analytics is understanding customer behavior. Many store owners focus on traffic and sales numbers but fail to dig deeper into what their customers are actually doing on their site. I've found that by leveraging behavioral analytics, store owners can gain powerful insights that allow them to optimize the shopping experience, increase conversions, and reduce friction. In this section, we'll explore how tools like heatmaps, session recordings, and cart abandonment tracking can provide invaluable insights into customer behavior. Additionally, we'll examine how identifying high-performing and underperforming products can lead to better business decisions.

Heatmaps and Session Recordings

Heatmaps and session recordings offer a visual representation of how customers interact with your website. When I first started using heatmaps, I was surprised at how much they revealed about user behavior that traditional analytics couldn't capture. A heatmap shows where users are clicking, scrolling, and spending the most time, while session recordings allow you to watch real users navigate your site in real-time.

I often recommend tools like Hotjar, Crazy Egg, and Lucky Orange to store owners looking to gain a deeper understanding of user experience. These tools highlight areas where customers get stuck, pages that receive the most engagement, and whether users are following the expected browsing patterns. For example, if a store's most important call-to-action button is in a cold zone (an area with little engagement), it's a clear sign that the design needs adjusting. Likewise, if a significant number of users drop off after reaching a specific section of a product page, it may indicate unclear messaging or a missing incentive to proceed further.

By reviewing session recordings, I've been able to help clients identify usability issues they would have otherwise overlooked. One client, for instance, had a checkout page with a lot of shipping options, many which were similar but different prices. Session recordings revealed that customers frequently scrolled up and down, seemingly looking for clarification, and many abandoned their carts shortly afterward. By removing redundant and unnecessary shipping options, they were able to achieve a noticeable drop in abandonment rates.

Cart Abandonment Tracking and Analysis

Cart abandonment is one of the biggest pain points in e-commerce, and almost every store owner has experienced frustration over customers who fill their carts only to leave without completing their purchase. I always tell my clients that understanding why customers abandon carts is the first step to fixing the problem.

By tracking cart abandonment through tools like Google Analytics, Shopify's or BigCommerce's built-in reports, or third-party apps like Klaviyo, store owners can identify patterns and potential obstacles in the checkout process. Common causes include unexpected shipping costs, mandatory account creation, or a long and complicated checkout flow. I've found that many customers simply get distracted and need a reminder, which is why automated abandoned cart email sequences are so effective.

A well-crafted abandoned cart email sequence should include a reminder of what's in the cart, a strong call-to-action, and potentially a small incentive like a discount or free shipping to encourage the customer to complete their purchase. I've seen businesses recover thousands of dollars in revenue simply by implementing a three-email sequence sent within 24 hours of abandonment.

Another strategy is offering exit-intent popups, which detect when a user is about to leave the site and present them with an offer or reminder. For example, one of my clients saw an immediate 15% decrease in cart abandonment rates after implementing an exit-intent discount popup on their cart page.

Identifying High-Performing vs. Underperforming Products

Another key to optimizing an e-commerce store is knowing which products are driving revenue and which are underperforming. Store owners often assume that their best-selling products are their most profitable ones, but this isn't always the case. By analyzing product performance data, businesses can make smarter decisions about inventory, promotions, and pricing.

I always advise looking at sales data, conversion rates, and profit margins together to get the full picture. A product might sell well but have low margins, making it less profitable than anticipated. Conversely, a product with a high conversion rate but low traffic might simply need better visibility to become a top seller.

I worked with a store owner who was struggling with slow-moving inventory. After reviewing their analytics, we identified that several underperforming products had high bounce rates on their product pages. Further investigation through heatmaps and session recordings revealed that many customers were leaving these pages due to a lack of clear product descriptions and images. By updating the product pages with better visuals and clearer descriptions, the store saw a 20% increase in conversions on those products within a month.

Additionally, it's important to track product seasonality and trends. Some products may have a natural sales cycle, meaning they should be promoted more aggressively at certain times of the year. Using historical sales data, store owners can predict when demand for certain products will spike and plan marketing efforts accordingly.

***

Understanding customer behavior through data is one of the most powerful ways to improve an e-commerce business. Heatmaps and session recordings provide insights into how users interact with your site, allowing for targeted design and usability improvements. Cart abandonment tracking helps pinpoint obstacles in the checkout process and provides opportunities to re-engage lost customers. Analyzing product performance ensures that store owners are focusing their efforts on the right inventory and maximizing profitability.

The key takeaway here is that data should drive decision-making, not your feelings. Rather than making assumptions about what's working and what isn't, store owners should rely on real user behavior to guide optimizations. When making decisions, stop and think whether you're making a choice based on what you want to be true, versus what the data actually shows. Likewise, if ego is playing any part in your decision-making, there's a good chance you're ignoring the metrics that really matter the most to your success.

In the next section, we'll explore how to leverage A/B testing to make data-backed improvements that lead to higher conversions and greater customer satisfaction.

USING DATA TO IMPROVE MARKETING CAMPAIGNS

One of the biggest advantages of running an online business is the ability to track and analyze marketing efforts in real time. Unlike traditional advertising, where results are often ambiguous, digital marketing provides a wealth of data that allows businesses to optimize their strategies, reduce wasted spending, and target the right audience more effectively. Over the years, I've worked with numerous e-commerce store owners who initially relied on intuition to guide their marketing efforts. Once they embraced data-driven strategies, their campaigns became far more efficient and profitable. In this section, I'll explore how A/B testing, email marketing segmentation, and personalized marketing can transform the way businesses connect with customers and drive sales.

A/B Testing Ads and Landing Pages

A/B testing, also known as split testing, is a fundamental practice for improving marketing performance. It involves testing two variations of an element – such as an advertisement, landing page, or email – to determine which performs better. This method eliminates guesswork and ensures marketing efforts are guided by actual user behavior.

When I first started testing ads, I was often surprised by the results. An ad I was certain would perform well sometimes fell flat, while a variation with a small tweak – such as a different call-to-action or image – would outperform it significantly. The key is to test systematically. I always recommend changing only one variable at a time, whether it's the headline, image, call-to-action, or offer, so that the impact of each change can be clearly measured.

Landing pages are another critical area where A/B testing makes a substantial difference. I once worked with an online retailer who struggled with a high bounce rate on their product pages. By A/B testing different elements – such as tweaking the layout, adjusting the placement of the "Buy Now" button, and simplifying the product description – we were able to improve conversion rates by 20% within a few weeks. Testing should be an ongoing process, as consumer preferences and behaviors shift over time.

Email Marketing Segmentation Using Data Insights

Email marketing remains one of the most effective channels for engaging customers, but a generic approach is rarely successful. Customers respond better when messages feel tailored to their interests and behaviors. This is where data-driven segmentation comes in.

When I first started working for Shoes.com, one of my primary responsibilities was managing the company's email marketing program. We implemented segmentation based on the links that subscribers clicked on – allowing us to determine if they were interested in men's, women's or children's shoes. We then sent different messages to each of those segments, improving engagement rates and conversion.

You can transform your email marketing results simply by breaking your audience into segments based on purchase history, browsing behavior, and engagement levels. For instance, a clothing retailer I consulted for initially sent the same email promotions to their entire list. By segmenting customers into groups – new subscribers, repeat buyers, and inactive customers – they were able to send more relevant content to each group. New subscribers received a welcome sequence with an introductory discount, repeat buyers got exclusive previews of new collections, and inactive customers were sent a re-engagement email with a special offer. This targeted approach led to a 35% increase in open rates and a significant boost in conversions.

Behavioral segmentation is another powerful tactic. If a customer frequently browses a particular category but hasn't made a purchase, sending them a targeted email featuring bestsellers from that category can be highly effective. Similarly, cart abandonment emails serve as a gentle nudge to remind customers of what they left behind, often recovering sales that would have otherwise been lost.

Personalizing Marketing Efforts Based on Customer Behavior

Personalization has moved beyond simply inserting a customer's first name in an email. Today, businesses can create deeply customized shopping experiences by leveraging behavioral data. I always emphasize to clients that the more relevant an offer or message feels to a customer, the more likely they are to engage with it.

One of the best examples of effective personalization comes from dynamic product recommendations. If a customer frequently purchases athletic gear, showing them similar products or suggesting complementary items – such as workout accessories or apparel – can increase order value. Many e-commerce platforms, including Shopify and BigCommerce, have built-in recommendation engines that use machine learning to analyze past purchases and browsing habits. Klaviyo also offers dynamic product widgets for email campaigns that are based on a customer's past shopping behavior.

Retargeting ads are another highly effective way

to personalize marketing. If a customer visits a product page but doesn't make a purchase, serving them an ad featuring that product (or similar items) can remind them to return and complete their purchase. I've worked with businesses that saw their return on ad spend double simply by implementing retargeting campaigns tailored to past visitor behavior.

Personalized customer journeys also extend to social media and live chat interactions. Many companies now use chatbots that provide tailored recommendations based on previous purchases or inquiries. Social media engagement can also be enhanced through personalized responses and targeted promotions based on customer demographics and past interactions.

***

Using data to refine marketing campaigns is one of the most powerful strategies an e-commerce business can adopt. A/B testing allows for continuous optimization, ensuring that ads and landing pages perform at their best. Email segmentation helps create targeted campaigns that resonate with different customer groups, increasing engagement and sales. Personalization takes marketing to the next level, delivering tailored experiences that enhance customer satisfaction and loyalty.

The most successful online businesses don't rely on guesswork – they use data to guide their decisions. By embracing analytics and continually testing and refining strategies, any e-commerce store can maximize the impact of its marketing efforts and drive long-term growth.

INVENTORY AND SALES FORECASTING WITH DATA

Managing inventory efficiently is one of the biggest challenges for e-commerce businesses. Too much stock can lead to excessive storage costs and markdowns, while too little can result in stockouts and lost revenue. Over the years, I've seen many startups struggle with inventory mismanagement simply because they weren't using their sales data effectively. Understanding sales trends, forecasting demand, and leveraging historical data can make a tremendous difference in maintaining the right balance of inventory. In this section, I'll explore how to predict demand, avoid stockouts, plan promotions, and interpret seasonal buying patterns to optimize inventory management.

How to Predict Demand and Avoid Stockouts

One of the first lessons I learned in e-commerce was that demand forecasting is never about guesswork – it's about using the right data. By analyzing past sales performance, businesses can predict which products are likely to sell well in the future and adjust their stock levels accordingly. This is particularly important for fast-moving products that tend to sell out quickly.

I worked with an online retailer who repeatedly ran out of stock on their most popular items. After reviewing their sales data, we identified clear purchasing trends that followed a monthly cycle. By adjusting their ordering schedule based on these insights, they were able to reduce stockouts by 40% within three months. The key takeaway? Patterns often exist in the data; you just have to know where to look.

Additionally, leveraging inventory management software that integrates with your e-commerce platform can automate much of this process. POS systems like Lightspeed or Heartland can help track stock levels in real-time and set reorder alerts when inventory dips below a certain threshold. Having an automated system in place reduces the likelihood of human error and ensures that store owners are always aware of stock needs.

If you're reliant on manufacturers or distributors who often go out of stock on key items, consider adding an "in-stock notification" tool to your product pages. These tools allow you to capture the email address of customers interested in the item, and then automatically notify them when the product returns to stock. Having these processes in place can earn you a sale that might have otherwise gone to a competitor.

Using Past Sales Data to Plan Promotions

Promotions can be a great way to drive sales, but they must be executed strategically. Too often, store owners launch discounts without analyzing past data, leading to either excess inventory they can't move or unexpected stockouts that frustrate customers. I always advise reviewing historical sales data before running a promotion to ensure there's enough stock available to meet demand.

One of my clients ran a Black Friday sale without analyzing past performance, only to sell out of their top-selling items within hours – leaving potential customers frustrated and revenue on the table. The next year, we took a different approach. By reviewing the previous year's sales trends, we identified which products saw the highest demand and preemptively increased stock levels. The result? A 35% increase in sales with fewer stockouts.

Analyzing sales history also helps determine the effectiveness of past promotions. By comparing sales figures before, during, and after a promotion, you can gauge whether it successfully boosted revenue or simply cannibalized future sales. For example, I once advised a store that noticed a drop in sales following their frequent flash sales. After reviewing their data, we discovered that customers were waiting for discounts before making purchases. To solve this, they adjusted their pricing strategy and limited promotional discounts, leading to steadier revenue growth.

Understanding Seasonal Trends and Buying Patterns

Seasonality plays a significant role in e-commerce, and recognizing these trends is essential for maintaining optimal inventory levels. I've seen too many businesses fail to anticipate seasonal fluctuations, leading to either excess stock they struggle to sell or missed opportunities due to understocking.

For instance, a swimwear retailer I worked with experienced an annual sales slump during the winter months. By analyzing their historical data, we identified a small but steady demand for resort wear and holiday travel gear during that time. By diversifying their product offerings and shifting marketing efforts to target vacationers, they were able to maintain sales during their traditionally slow season.

Another common mistake I see is businesses failing to prepare for peak seasons. Many industries see a surge in sales during holidays like Christmas, back-to-school periods, or summer vacations. By reviewing sales data from previous years, businesses can predict when demand will spike and ensure they have the right stock levels in place. Preordering seasonal inventory based on past sales trends can help prevent supply chain delays and missed sales opportunities.

Additionally, buying patterns vary based on customer demographics. For example, younger audiences may respond well to limited-time drops and fast fashion trends, while older demographics may have more consistent buying habits. Analyzing customer segments within sales data can help tailor inventory planning to meet the specific needs of your audience.

***

Inventory and sales forecasting are essential for running a successful e-commerce business. Predicting demand using past sales data helps avoid costly stockouts, while planning promotions based on historical performance ensures that discounting strategies drive revenue rather than hinder future sales. Recognizing seasonal trends allows businesses to maintain steady revenue flow and optimize inventory levels throughout the year.

E-commerce can move quickly, but data gives business owners the power to stay ahead of demand fluctuations. By leveraging analytics and inventory management tools, businesses can make informed decisions that prevent lost revenue and improve overall efficiency. In the next section, we'll explore how automation can further streamline inventory tracking and fulfillment processes, making operations smoother and more scalable.

AUTOMATING ANALYTICS FOR SMARTER DECISION-MAKING

One of the biggest breakthroughs in e-commerce over the past few years has been the ability to automate analytics and reporting. When I first started analyzing e-commerce data, I spent hours manually pulling reports, comparing spreadsheets, and trying to spot trends. It was a slow and inefficient process. Today, automation tools can do this work in minutes, allowing business owners to focus on interpreting data and making informed decisions rather than getting lost in tedious calculations. In this section, I'll explore the most effective tools for automating analytics, the power of AI-driven recommendations, and when to rely on experts versus DIY solutions.

Tools for Automating Reports and Insights

The ability to access real-time data without manual effort is a game-changer for e-commerce businesses. I often recommend tools like Google

Analytics, Shopify Reports, and BigCommerce Insights for built-in reporting features. These platforms allow you to track sales trends, customer behavior, and website performance with minimal setup. However, for businesses that require deeper insights, more advanced solutions like Looker, Tableau, and Power BI offer powerful data visualization and automation capabilities.

One of my favorite automation tools is Google Data Studio, which allows you to create custom dashboards that pull data from multiple sources in real time. By setting up an automated dashboard in Google Data Studio, you can instantly see sales performance across all platforms in one place, leading to better-informed marketing and inventory decisions. Glew is another analytics tool that can pull data from multiple sources and create automatic reports that are emailed to you daily, weekly or monthly.

Another useful tool is Klaviyo, which not only provides email marketing automation but also tracks customer lifetime value, repeat purchase rates, and segmentation trends. Instead of manually sorting through email campaign data, business owners can utilize Klaviyo's analytics to pinpoint which audiences are most engaged and adjust their messaging accordingly.

AI-Driven Analytics and Recommendations

Artificial intelligence has revolutionized e-commerce analytics, making it easier than ever to uncover patterns and optimize business strategies. AI-driven tools use machine learning to predict customer behavior, recommend pricing adjustments, and suggest inventory restocking before stockouts occur. One of the most impressive applications of AI I've seen is dynamic pricing software, such as Prisync or Wiser, which automatically adjusts product prices based on competitor activity and demand fluctuations.

AI-powered customer segmentation is another powerful feature that allows businesses to personalize their marketing efforts at scale. Instead of manually sorting customers into different groups, AI analyzes purchase behavior, browsing history, and engagement levels to create highly targeted audience segments.

Predictive analytics is also a growing trend in e-commerce. AI can analyze past purchasing patterns to forecast future demand, helping businesses optimize stock levels and plan for seasonal shifts. I've seen businesses use predictive analytics to avoid over-ordering slow-moving inventory while ensuring that bestsellers are always in stock.

When to Hire an Expert vs. Using DIY Tools

With so many automation tools available, the

question often arises: when should you manage analytics on your own, and when is it time to hire an expert? From my experience, it depends on the complexity of your business and your comfort level with data analysis.

For small businesses with straightforward operations, DIY tools like Shopify Analytics or Google Analytics often provide enough insights to make informed decisions. Many platforms offer plug-and-play integrations that make it easy to track sales, traffic sources, and customer trends without needing advanced expertise. If your main goal is monitoring basic metrics like conversion rates, average order value, and email open rates, automation tools can handle most of the heavy lifting.

However, as businesses scale, the need for more advanced analytics often grows. I've worked with companies that reached a point where they needed deeper insights, such as identifying profitability by SKU, optimizing multi-channel advertising spend, or predicting churn rates. At this stage, hiring a data analyst or consultant can be a worthwhile investment. Professionals can help set up more sophisticated tracking systems, customize reports, and interpret data in ways that automation tools might miss.

Another case where expert assistance is beneficial is when setting up complex dashboards or integrating multiple data sources. Bringing in an expert to consolidate and automate this data can save you hours of work each week and lead to more accurate business strategies.

***

Automating analytics is one of the most effective ways for e-commerce businesses to stay ahead of their competitors. With the right tools, store owners can track performance metrics effortlessly, uncover valuable insights through AI-driven recommendations, and make data-backed decisions without getting bogged down by spreadsheets. While DIY tools are excellent for small businesses, growing brands may benefit from hiring experts to take their analytics to the next level. As technology continues to evolve, leveraging automation will become even more critical for staying competitive.

FINAL THOUGHTS & NEXT STEPS

As we come to the end of this book, I want to emphasize just how transformative analytics can be when applied effectively. Over the years, I've worked with countless businesses that initially relied on intuition to make decisions. While gut feelings and experience are valuable, I know from experience that those who embrace data gain a significant competitive edge. Understanding customer behavior, optimizing marketing strategies, managing inventory efficiently, and leveraging automation all contribute to the long-term e-commerce success.

Summary of Key Takeaways

Looking back at what we've covered, several themes stand out. First, data is the foundation of smart decision-making in e-commerce. Without tracking and analyzing key performance indicators, businesses operate in the dark, making it difficult to grow sustainably. We explored how businesses can use tools like Google Analytics, Shopify Reports, and AI-driven analytics to extract meaningful insights from raw numbers.

Another major takeaway is the power of understanding customer behavior. By using heatmaps, session recordings, and cart abandonment tracking, businesses can refine the user experience and remove roadblocks that prevent conversions. I've seen businesses increase their sales simply by making small adjustments, such as repositioning a call-to-action button or streamlining the checkout process.

Marketing optimization is another component of success. Through A/B testing, email segmentation, and personalized marketing, businesses can ensure that their campaigns reach the right audience with the right message. I've worked with store owners who slashed their ad spend while increasing revenue just by refining their targeting based on real customer data.

Inventory management and sales forecasting were also key topics. Using past sales data to predict demand and avoid stockouts is one of the most effective ways to ensure profitability. Many businesses struggle with either overstocking or running out of bestsellers, but by analyzing trends and seasonal buying patterns, they can find the right balance.

Finally, we explored automation and AI-driven analytics. The ability to streamline data collection, reporting, and predictive analysis saves time and allows business owners to focus on strategy rather than tedious number-crunching. Whether it's using

AI to adjust pricing dynamically or implementing automated reports for real-time insights, businesses that embrace automation can scale more efficiently.

How to Create a Data-Driven Action Plan

Now that we've covered these key areas, the next step is putting the knowledge into action. I always recommend starting with an audit of your current data collection processes. What tools are you already using, and are they set up correctly? Are you focusing on the right metrics, or are you drowning in data without clear insights? Taking stock of where you are will help you identify gaps that need to be addressed.

Once you have a clear picture of your existing data infrastructure, set measurable goals based on what you've learned. If your conversion rates are lower than industry benchmarks, start by identifying where users drop off in the sales funnel and experiment with solutions. If your inventory levels are inconsistent, implement forecasting methods based on past trends.

Consistency is key. Data analysis isn't a one-time exercise – it's an ongoing process. Make it a habit to review reports weekly or monthly, depending on the volume of transactions in your store. I often advise businesses to set up automated dashboards that provide real-time insights, ensuring they can react to changes quickly. But it's not enough to set them up – you have to actually look at them!

Testing and iteration should also be part of your plan. Whether it's refining marketing campaigns or tweaking your website's user experience, using data to guide incremental improvements can lead to significant results over time. Many successful businesses treat every decision as an experiment, tracking outcomes and refining their approach based on performance data.

Leveraging Expert Advice for Continued Growth

While DIY analytics tools are powerful, there comes a point where outside expertise can make a world of difference. I've worked with store owners who initially managed their data analysis on their own but eventually realized that bringing in an expert helped them unlock insights they would have otherwise missed. Data consultants, marketing analysts, and inventory management specialists can help set up more advanced tracking systems, interpret complex trends, and optimize business operations at a deeper level.

For example, if you're struggling with attribution – figuring out which marketing channels are driving the most sales – an expert can help implement more sophisticated tracking solutions beyond what basic analytics tools offer. If you want to dive into AI-powered demand forecasting, hiring a specialist to set up predictive modeling can save you months of trial and error.

Beyond consultants, networking with other e-commerce professionals can be incredibly valuable. Joining industry groups, attending conferences, or participating in online forums can expose you to best practices and new technologies that keep you ahead of the competition. I've personally learned some of my best growth strategies just by working with a wide variety of e-commerce clients over the years.

Final Words

E-commerce businesses that thrive are the ones that leverage data to stay ahead of trends. Whether you're just starting or scaling up an established store, integrating data-driven decision-making into every aspect of your business will ensure long-term growth and success. It's not about chasing numbers – it's about using insights to make strategic, informed choices that lead to sustainable profitability.

If you take one thing away from this book, let it be this: Data isn't just a tool – it's a roadmap. The more effectively you use it, the clearer your path to success becomes. By putting your insights into action, you'll see your e-commerce business grow in ways you never imagined.

ABOUT THE AUTHOR

Danielle Mead

Danielle Mead is an e-commerce expert with over 25 years of experience working at dotcom startups and as an independent web designer and consultant. She has worked with over 600 clients across industries to launch and optimize online stores that deliver results. Her one-woman company, Duck Soup E-Commerce, primarily works with clients on the BigCommerce platform, empowering online retailers with practical tools and strategies to overcome challenges and succeed in competitive markets. She is passionate about simplifying the complexities of e-commerce and creating clear, actionable plans for success. Learn more about Danielle and her services at her website https://ducksoupecommerce.com.

www.ingramcontent.com/pod-product-compliance
Lightning Source LLC
LaVergne TN
LVHW051624050326
832903LV00033B/4651

* 9 7 9 8 3 1 4 9 7 3 0 0 4 *